Sea Life

Hermit Crabs

Lola Schaefer

 Raintree

www.raintreepublishers.co.uk
Visit our website to find out more information about **Raintree** books.

To order:

 Phone 44 (0) 1865 888112

 Send a fax to 44 (0) 1865 314091

Visit the Raintree Bookshop at www.raintreepublishers.co.uk to browse our catalogue and order online.

First published in Great Britain by Raintree, Halley Court, Jordan Hill, Oxford OX2 8EJ, part of Harcourt Education.
Raintree is a registered trademark of Harcourt Education Ltd.

Editorial: Nick Hunter and Diyan Leake
Design: Sue Emerson (HL-US) and Joanna Sapwell (www.tipani.co.uk)
Picture Research: Amor Montes de Oca (HL-US)
Production: Lorraine Hicks

Originated by Dot Gradations
Printed and bound in China by South China Printing Company

ISBN 1 844 21011 1
07 06 05 04 03
10 9 8 7 6 5 4 3 2 1

 CAUTION: Remind children that it is not a good idea to handle wild animals. Children should wash their hands with soap and water after they touch any animal.

British Library Cataloguing in Publication Data
Schaefer, Lola
Hermit Crabs
595.3'87
A full catalogue record for this book is available from the British Library.

Acknowledgements
The publishers would like to thank the following for permission to reproduce photographs: C. B. & D. W. Frith pp. **20**, **23** (female); Color Pic, Inc. p. **16** (E. R. Degginger); David Liebman pp. **7**, **11**; Doug Perrine p. **1**; Dwight Kuhn p. **4**; Eda Rogers p. **14**; Jay Ireland & Georgienne E. Bradley/Bradleyireland.com pp. **15L**, **18**, **19**; Jeff Rotman Photography pp. **8**, **12**, **13**, **15R**, **23** (claw, eyestalk, seaweed), back cover (eyestalk); Kazunari Kawashima p. **21**; Rob and Ann Simpson pp. **10**, **22**, **24**; Seapics.com p. **17** (Richard Hermann), **23** (jointed leg, Richard Hermann), back cover (jointed leg, Richard Hermann); Visuals Unlimited pp. **5** (Kjell B. Sandved), **6** (James Beveridge), **9** (Glenn M. Oliver), **23** (antennae, Glenn M. Oliver; invertebrate, Kjell B. Sandved)

Cover photograph of a hermit crab, reproduced with permission of Jeff Rotman Photography

Every effort has been made to contact copyright holders of any material reproduced in this book. Any omissions will be rectified in subsequent printings if notice is given to the publishers.

Some words are shown in bold, **like this**. You can find them in the glossary on page 23.

Contents

What are hermit crabs?

Hermit crabs are small animals.

They are hard on the outside.

They do not have any bones inside.

jointed leg

claw

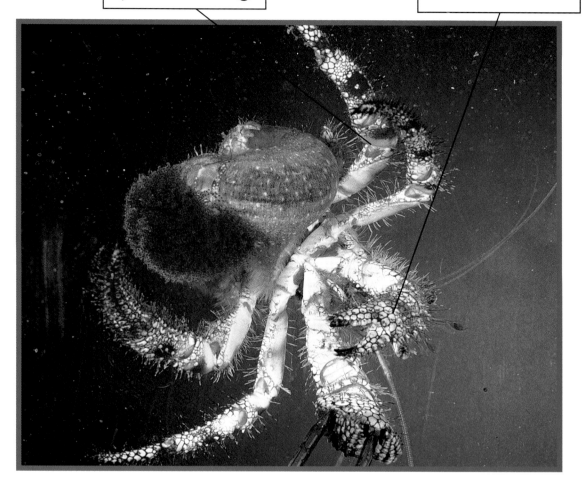

Animals that do not have backbones are called **invertebrates**.

Hermit crabs are invertebrates with **claws** and **jointed legs.**

Where do hermit crabs live?

Some hermit crabs live on the sand at the seaside.

Others live in the sea.

old shell

Hermit crabs live in shells.

When hermit crabs grow, they move to bigger shells.

What is on a hermit crab's head?

eyestalks

Hermit crabs have two **eyestalks** on their head.

They also have four **antennae**.

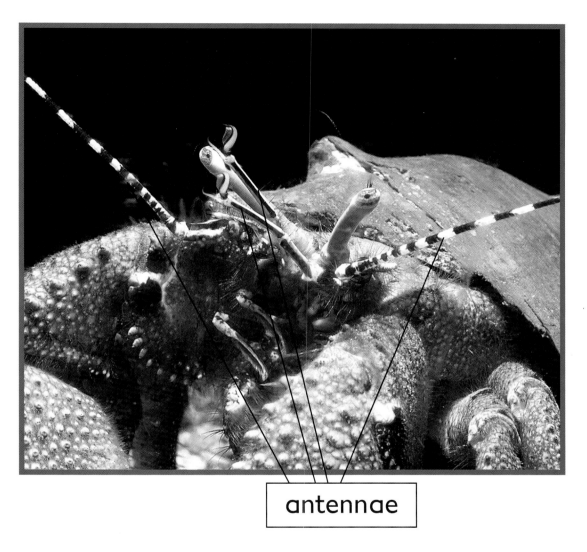

antennae

Hermit crabs use their antennae to feel and smell things.

What are hermit crab shells like?

Hermit crabs do not have their own shells.

They grow a hard cover on their bodies.

Hermit crabs take the empty shells of other animals.

Then they carry them as if they were their own shells.

What do hermit crabs feel like?

Hermit crabs feel rough.

The shells they carry are hard.

claw

Hermit crab **claws** are sharp.

How big are hermit crabs?

Young hermit crabs are smaller than a fingernail.

Some adult hermit crabs are small enough to fit in your hand.

Some are as large as a tennis ball.

How do hermit crabs move?

Young hermit crabs swim.

Adult hermit crabs crawl.

Hermit crabs can crawl up, down and sideways.

They can even crawl over each other.

What do hermit crabs eat?

seaweed

Hermit crabs eat plants and animals.

They eat leaves and **seaweed**.

Hermit crabs eat tiny sea animals.

They even eat dead animals on the sand.

Where do new hermit crabs come from?

eggs

Female hermit crabs lay thousands of eggs.

They stick the eggs on their bodies.

eggs

They shake the eggs into the sea.

Young hermit crabs come out of the eggs.

Quiz

What are these hermit crab parts?

Can you find them in the book?

Look for the answers on page 24.

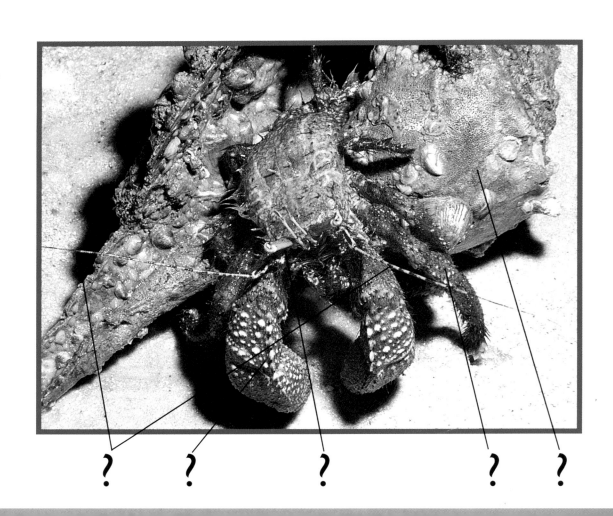

? ? ? ? ?

Glossary

antennae
long parts on an animal's head that it uses as feelers

claw
part that a crab uses to hold things with, like a hand

eyestalk
long part on a crab's head where its eyes are

female
girl or mother

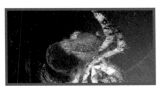

invertebrate
animal that has no backbone

jointed leg
leg with parts that move where they are joined together

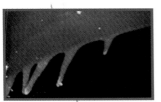

seaweed
plant that lives in the sea

Index

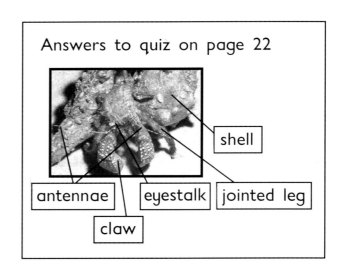

Answers to quiz on page 22

shell

antennae   eyestalk   jointed leg

claw

Titles in the Sea Life series include:

Hardback   1 844 21010 3

Hardback   1 844 21011 1

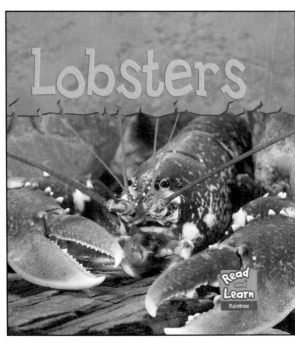

Hardback   1 844 21012 X

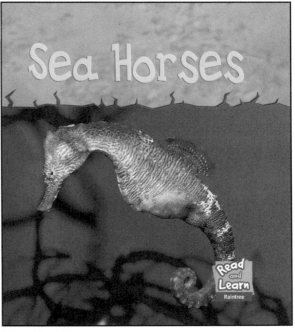

Hardback   1 844 21013 8

Find out about the other titles in this series on our website www.raintreepublishers.co.uk